LAUGH OUT LOUD!

THE SCHOOL'S COOL JOKE BOOK

Sean Connolly and Kay Barnham

W

FRANKLIN WATTS
LONDON • SYDNEY

First published in 2012 by Franklin Watts

Copyright © 2012 Arcturus Publishing Limited

Franklin Watts
338 Euston Road
London
NW1 3BH

Franklin Watts Australia
Level 17/207 Kent Street, Sydney, NSW 2000

Produced by Arcturus Publishing Limited,
26/27 Bickels Yard, 151–153 Bermondsey Street, London SE1 3HA

Editor: Joe Harris
Illustrations: Adam Clay and Dynamo Design
Layout Design: Notion Design

A CIP catalogue record for this book is available from the British Library.

Dewey Decimal Classification Number: 818.6'02-dc23

ISBN: 978 1 4451 1494 1

Franklin Watts is a division of Hachette Children's Books, an Hachette UK company.
www.hachette.co.uk

Printed in China

SL001837EN
Supplier 03, Date 0512, Print Run 1965

CONTENTS

Jokes...................................... 4

Glossary................................... 32

Index...................................... 32

Further Reading............................ 32

Websites................................... 32

What was the dentist's favourite subject at school?
Flossophy.

What did the number 0 say to the number 8?
'That's a cool belt.'

What do you get if you cross a vampire and a teacher?
Blood tests.

Why did the teacher wear sunglasses?
Because his class was so bright.

Why did the teacher jump into the swimming pool?
He wanted to test the water.

What kind of lunches do geometry teachers enjoy?
Square meals.

Head: You'll start with a salary of £25,000 and then go up to £35,000 in six months.
Teacher: In that case I think I would like to start in six months!

Why was the cross-eyed teacher's class rioting?
She couldn't control her pupils.

Why was the broom late for school?
It overswept.

Teacher: Who invented King Arthur's round table?
Pupil: Was it Sir Cumference?

Did you hear about the cannibal that was expelled from school?
He was buttering up the teachers.

Teacher: What language do they speak in Cuba?
Pupil: Cubic!

Why did one pencil tell the other pencil that it looked old and tired?
Because it was blunt.

What's the tastiest class at school?
History. It's full of dates.

My music teacher said I have a heavenly voice!
That's not strictly true – she said your voice was like nothing on Earth!

Teacher: You missed school yesterday, didn't you?
Pupil: Not very much!

Why did the pupil think the teacher had a crush on him?
She put 'X's all over his homework.

Teacher: Why are you taking that sponge into class?
Pupil: Because I find your classes so absorbing!

What is a polygon?
A dead parrot.

Why was the maths textbook miserable?
It had too many problems.

SCHOOL'S COOL

Why was the music teacher locked out of his classroom?
The keys were on the piano.

English teacher: Give me an example of a long sentence.
Pupil: Life imprisonment.

What did the pencil say to the protractor?
Take me to your ruler.

I sprained my ankle and had to miss PE for 2 weeks.
Lucky you. Our PE teacher never accepts a lame excuse for his class!

Why don't leopards bother to cheat in exams?
Because they know that they will always be spotted!

Is the maths teacher in
a good mood today?
I wouldn't count on it!

Teacher: Can you
define the word
'hardship'?
Pupil: Is it a boat made
out of concrete?

My maths teacher is
a real peach!
You mean she's
pretty?
No – I mean she has a heart of stone!

What do history teachers do before they get married?
They go out on dates!

Why is 6 afraid of 7?
Because 7 ate 9!

Parent: Why have you given my son such a bad grade in his report? He's as intelligent as the next boy!

Teacher: Yes, but the next boy is an idiot!

Teacher: Eat up your school lunch – it's full of iron.

Pupil: That explains why it's so difficult to chew!

Teacher: How did people spend their time in the Stone Age?

Pupil: Did they listen to rock music?

Parent: Do you think my son has what it takes to be a pilot?

Teacher: Well, he certainly spends plenty of time with his head in the clouds!

What happens when music teachers are sick?
They send in a note!

Why was the archaeology teacher unhappy?
Her career was in ruins.

History teacher: How would you discover what life in Ancient Egypt was really like?
Pupil: I'd ask my mummy!

Did you hear about the maths teacher whose mistakes started to multiply?
In the end, they had to take him away!

Why does your teacher have her hair in a bun?
Because she has a face like a burger!

Teacher: What is the plural of baby?
Pupil: Twins!

Why do nursery teachers have such a positive attitude?
They know how to make the little things count.

Parent: Do you think my son will make a good
Arctic explorer?
Teacher: I would think so – most of his grades are
below zero!

Teacher: Can you tell me what water is?

Pupil: It's a colourless liquid
that turns black when I put
my hands in it!

Why is that boy locked up in a
cage in the corner of the
classroom?
Oh, he's the teacher's pet!

12

I think our school must be haunted.
Why?
Because the head teacher keeps talking about the school spirit!

Teacher: Who discovered Pluto?
Pupil: Walt Disney!

Teacher: What do Attila the Hun and Winnie the Pooh have in common?
Pupil: They have the same middle name!

Teacher: Michael, how do we know that the Earth is round?
Michael: I didn't say it was, Mr Johnson!

Teacher: If you multiply 245 by 3,456 and divide the answer by 165, then subtract 752, what will you get?
Pupil: The wrong answer!

Teacher: How good are you at picking up music?
Pupil: Well, I'm not sure if I could lift a whole piano!

Teacher: Jessica, how did you find the questions in your English test?
Jessica: Oh, I found the questions easily enough – it's the answers I couldn't find!

Teacher: Please don't talk while you are doing your exam.
Pupil: It's all right, Miss Brown. We're not doing the exam – just talking!

Teacher: Who invented fractions?
Pupil: Henry the Eighth!

Where do vampire schoolchildren go on school trips?
Lake Eerie!

How does a maths teacher remove wax from his ears?
He works it out with a pencil!

Teacher: Why were you late this morning, Katie?
Katie: I squeezed the toothpaste too hard, and it took me
half an hour to get it all back into the tube again!

Pupil: Can we do some work on the Iron Age today?
Teacher: Well, I'm not certain, I'm a bit rusty on that
period of history!

Teacher: Ten cats were
at the cinema. One
walked out. How many
were left?
Pupil: None – they were
all copycats!

Teacher: What's a
computer byte?
Pupil: I didn't even know
they had teeth!

What happened after the wheel was first invented?
It caused a revolution!

Teacher: Did you know that most accidents happen in the kitchen?
Pupil: Yes, but we still have to eat them!

Mum: Time to get up and go to school!
Son: I don't want to go! Everyone hates me and I get bullied!
Mum: But you have to go – you're the head teacher!

Teacher: How many seconds are there in a year?
Pupil: Twelve – January 2nd, February 2nd...

What did the music teacher need a ladder for?
Reaching the high notes!

I banged my head on the classroom door this morning!
Have you seen the school nurse?
No, just stars!

Teacher: Why is your homework late?
Pupil: Sorry, Miss Elliot, my dad is a slow writer!

Maths teacher: What are net profits?
Pupil: What fishermen have left after paying the crew!

I'm not really interested in maths: I just go along to the lesson to make up the numbers!

Teacher: How do archaeologists get into locked tombs?
Pupil: Do they use a skeleton key?

What was the blackbird doing in the school library?
Looking for bookworms!

Did you hear about the PE teacher who used to run around the classroom in order to jog pupils' memories?

Why did the school orchestra have such awful manners?
Because it didn't know how to conduct itself!

Teacher: In the future, all trains and buses will run on time.
Pupil: Won't they run on fuel, just like now?

Teacher: I wish you'd pay a little attention!
Pupil: I'm paying as little as I can!

Teacher: How did people react when electricity was first discovered?
Pupil: They got a nasty shock!

Young man, I hope I don't catch you cheating in the maths test!
So do I, Miss Goldman!

What is a science teacher's favourite breed of dog?
A lab!

When do 2 and 2 make more than 4?
When they make 22!

Sign outside the music department:
Violin for sale. Good price – no strings attached!

SCHOOL'S COOL

Teacher: Why was the invention of the safety match an important change?
Pupil: It was a striking achievement!

Why did the school cafeteria hire a dentist?
To make more filling meals!

Parent: Do you think my son could work as a DJ on the radio?
Teacher: He certainly has the face for it!

Why are teachers good at pool?
Because they always bring their own chalk!

How do you know your school bus is old?
The seats are covered in mammoth hide!

Why did the burglar
break into the music
department?
He was after the lute!

Why was Cinderella
terrible at sports?
Because her coach
was a pumpkin!

Did you hear about the
maths teacher and the
art teacher who used to go out together?
They spent their time painting by numbers!

Teacher: This homework looks as though it has been
written by your father.
Pupil: Of course it does – I borrowed his pen!

Teacher: Which two words in the English language have
the most letters?
Pupil: 'Post Office!'

Teacher: Where were all the kings and queens of France crowned?
Pupil: On the head!

Teacher: Which age did the mummies live in?
Pupil: The Band-Age!

Where did King Arthur's men get their training?
At knight school!

What were the 16 schoolboys playing in the telephone box?
Squash!

What sort of ring is always square?
A boxing ring!

How many librarians does it take to change a lightbulb?
Two. One to screw it in and one to say, 'Shhhhhhh!' at the squeaking noise.

Book seen in the school library:
The Survivors' Guide to Escaping from a Sinking Ship by Mandy Lifeboats

What do you say to the school's best pole vaulter?
Hiya!

Geography teacher: Where is the English Channel?
Pupil: I don't know, my TV doesn't have that one!

Why did the silly pupil buy a seahorse?
Because he wanted to play water polo!

23

Mum: Why didn't you come straight home from school?
Daughter: Because we live around the corner!

Where do you find a giant scholar?
Around the neck of a giant's shirt.

In a family with seven children, why was the youngest late for school?
The alarm was set for six.

Which tables don't they teach you in maths class?
Dinner tables.

History teacher: Which famous knight never won a single battle?
Pupil: Sir Endor!

SCHOOL'S COOL

Teacher: What was Robin Hood's mum called?
Pupil: Mother Hood.

Teacher: What is the plural of mouse?
Pupil: Mice!
Teacher: And what is the plural of house?
Pupil: Hice!

What's the difference between a train and a teacher?
A train says, 'Choo choo!' but a teacher says, 'Take that gum out of your mouth this instant!'

What did the IT teacher name his baby son?
Chip.

Teacher: What is a myth?
Pupil: A female moth!

Teacher: Our school cafeteria is spotlessly clean.
Pupil: Is that why the food always tastes of soap?

Teacher: How do you make a sick insect better?
Pupil: Give it a 'T', then it will be a stick insect!

Geography teacher: Jack, where is Turkey?
Jack: No idea, sir, I haven't seen it since Christmas!

Music teacher: What sort of music can you make with your feet?
Pupil: Sole music!

Why did the school cook become a history teacher?
She was an expert on ancient grease!

What happens to old French teachers?
One day they realize that un oeuf is enough!

Well, son, how did you find your geography test?
With a map and compass – how else!

Teacher: I think you need glasses.
Pupil: What makes you think that, Mr Adams?
Teacher: You're facing the wrong way!

Today is flying saucer day at the school cafeteria.
How come?
Because we get unidentified frying objects!

SCHOOL'S COOL

Teacher: If I gave you £10 a week for the next six months what would you have?
Pupil: A crazy teacher!

English teacher: For tonight's homework I want you to write an essay on Moby Dick.
Pupil: I can't do that, Miss Schneider!
Teacher: Why on earth not?
Pupil: I don't have any waterproof ink!

Why did the cyclops have to retire from teaching?
He only had one pupil!

What is a maths teacher's favourite dessert?
Apple pi.

Music teacher: What do you get if you drop a piano down a mineshaft?
Pupil: A flat minor!

Teacher: Which part of a fish weighs the most?
Pupil: The scales!

Science teacher: Why do doctors and nurses wear masks in the hospital operating room?
Pupil: So if they make a mistake, no one will know who did it!

Teacher: Did your mum or dad help you with these questions?
Pupil: No, I got them wrong all by myself!

Science teacher: Fred, what food do giraffes eat?
Pupil: Neck-tarines!

Teacher: Why were you late for school today?
Pupil: I got a flat tyre on my bicycle.
Teacher: Did you run over some broken glass?
Pupil: No, there was a fork in the road!

History teacher: Why was the guillotine invented?
Pupil: As a cure for dandruff?

Why did the flea get expelled from flea school?
He just wasn't up to scratch!

Teacher: In this exam you will be allowed 15 minutes for each question.
Pupil: How long do we get for the answers?

Science teacher: Harry, how would you fix a short circuit?
Harry: Add some more wire to make it longer?

Geography teacher: Amy, what can you tell me about the Dead Sea?
Amy: I didn't even know it was sick!

Teacher: Where is the easiest place to find diamonds?
Pupil: In a deck of cards!

I've always had a hard time with decimals – I just can't see the point!

Pupil: I don't think I deserved a zero in this test.
Teacher: I agree – but it's the lowest mark I could give you!

Teacher: Why are you doing your multiplication on the floor?
Pupil: You told me not to use tables.

How did the school orchestra leader survive being hit by lightning?
He was a very bad conductor!

Glossary

archaeology the study of ancient remains

byte a measurement of information on a computer

geometry an area of maths concerned with shapes

guillotine a machine for cutting off heads that was used in the French Revolution

mineshaft a long tunnel that leads into a mine

protractor a tool for measuring angles

Further Reading

Editors of Usborne. *School Jokes*. Usborne Publishing, 2003.

Howell, Laura. *The Usborne Book of Really Awful Jokes About School and Other Stuff*. Usborne Publishing, 2005.

Winter, Judy. *Jokes About School*. Pebble Books, 2010.

Index

cafeterias 20, 26, 27
English 8, 14, 28
exams 8, 14, 30
geography 26, 27, 30
history 5, 6, 9, 10, 11, 15, 22, 24, 27, 30
homework 7, 17, 21, 28
libraries 18, 23
maths 5, 7, 9, 11, 13, 14, 15, 16, 17, 19, 21, 24, 28, 31
music 7, 8, 10, 11, 14, 16, 18, 19, 21, 26, 28, 31
pencils 6, 8, 15
science 19, 29, 30
tests 4, 14, 19, 27, 31

Websites

CBBC 'Crack a Joke' game: *www.bbc.co.uk/cbbc/shows/cbbc-jokes*

Jokes by Kids website: *www.jokesbykids.com*

Yahoo! Kids Jokes: *http://kids.yahoo.com/jokes*